Lo

A Preacher's STRUGGLE

How the Dynamics of Rejections Lead
to the Greatest Battle of My Life

TATE PUBLISHING
AND ENTERPRISES, LLC

A Preacher's Struggle
Copyright © 2015 by Louis Collins. All rights reserved.

No part of this publication may be reproduced, stored in a retrieval system or transmitted in any way by any means, electronic, mechanical, photocopy, recording or otherwise without the prior permission of the author except as provided by USA copyright law.

This book is designed to provide accurate and authoritative information with regard to the subject matter covered. This information is given with the understanding that neither the author nor Tate Publishing, LLC is engaged in rendering legal, professional advice. Since the details of your situation are fact dependent, you should additionally seek the services of a competent professional. The opinions expressed by the author are not necessarily those of Tate Publishing, LLC.

Published by Tate Publishing & Enterprises, LLC
127 E. Trade Center Terrace | Mustang, Oklahoma 73064 USA
1.888.361.9473 | www.tatepublishing.com

Tate Publishing is committed to excellence in the publishing industry. The company reflects the philosophy established by the founders, based on Psalm 68:11,
"The Lord gave the word and great was the company of those who published it."

Book design copyright © 2015 by Tate Publishing, LLC. All rights reserved.
Cover design by Errol Villamante
Interior design by Mary Jean Archival
Photos taken by Christian Hicks

Published in the United States of America

ISBN: 978-1-63418-790-9
1. Biography & Autobiography / Religious
2. Self-Help / Personal Growth / Self-Esteem
14.11.24

A Preacher's STRUGGLE

To my loving family for always believing in me and supporting my goals in life

To Pastor Herman Hicks. Thanks for your willingness to take a chance on a young stubborn preacher who needed guidance

And to mentors and friends along the way, thank you!

Patrick Green, C. J. Luckey (Brothers from another mother)

Stephanie Street (My heart and soul)

and my Central Christian College family

Contents

Introduction 9
Family Affair 11
A Loose Canon and Puppy Love 21
The Loner Meets His Bestest 27
Sold Out, the Church Boy Experience 41
My First Time 51
Sold Out, the Playboy Experience 63
Stole My Heart 67
God Blocked It 77
Alone 81
Struggle Turned Testimony 89
Epilogue 95
Contact 99

Introduction

Let me be clear that though the title of my book is *A Preacher's Struggle*, it is definitely not intended for preachers or people in ministry alone, nor is it a story that glorifies the struggle with sex addiction. The story is about a young man's battle that almost takes his life, integrity, and good character to the brink of total destruction. Everyone either has or has had a demonic force that they had to war against. The issue is that when we refuse to deal with problems in our lives early enough, we face the consequences of having them surface in other areas in our life. Coupled with that, we then try to figure out why we carry out certain unhealthy actions in our lives and almost all the time, it points to an incident, problem, or heretical curse that we refused to face head on. When we suppress our problems, they ultimately suffocate us.

I believe prominent preachers and church leaders have found themselves being ousted by a problem that they refused to get help for, and it eventually damaged or destroyed their ministry altogether. All sicknesses are not carnal, and the worst thing a person can do is be in denial about problems that they know are having a direct effect on their lives and the people around them. It is important that people tell their own story. When an individual tells their own story, they remove the people who have motives to sabotage your future and assassinate your character. No one will be able to tell your story like you can, so travel with me as I let you in to mine.

Family Affair

Born in the greatest city in America, Los Angeles, California, I loved the ocean breeze, the tall palm trees, and the sunny weather. Yes, the beautiful image most people see when they think of the City of Angels. Yet for me and my family, the picture was slightly different.

Between the ages of birth and seven years old, my two sisters Latoya and Debrea (Latoya being the oldest of the children) and I lived with my grandparents in the heart of South Central Los Angeles. My grandparents stayed in a small three-bedroom house and their sister (my aunt) who lived behind them. I became really close to my grandmother.

My grandmother was probably the sole reason I stayed inside a lot because I did not want to be around anyone but her. My mother and father were married at the time but were still trying to figure a lot of things out. They married young. When my mother married, she was actually pregnant with my oldest sister.

My whole family for the most part was really close-knit. I applaud my uncles and aunts for doing the best they could to keep me and my cousins close and have family events and gatherings. In fact, one of the closest, if not the closest, person to me is my cousin Andrea. I believe from birth, she and I were designed for each other. There was no other cousin I got more excited about coming to family events.

Even as an adult now, we would do anything for each other no matter what it came to. However it was my only two male cousins (on my mother side) who taught me how to be a boy. In fact, they picked on me so much in competitive games that they are the reason today that I hate to lose at anything. Things did change drastically as I got older, and they began to realize that I was going to be bigger than the both of them and more gifted athletically that they stopped messing with me.

Even with all that said, for me and my siblings, we resented all of our cousins. For much of our adolescent years and even into our teens, my sisters and I felt like the outcast. This is largely due to the fact that we became the victims of a broken home.

While we were still fairly young, my mother and father moved my sisters and I out to Pomona, California. It was still in the Los Angeles County but about thirty minutes east of South Central. It wasn't that much better than where we previously lived but good enough for my family to make a fresh start away from my grandparents. I hated that house.

For many years of my life I lived in roach-infested places with broken appliances and furniture that was terrible-looking and falling apart. Still, nothing compared to this house because it was the place that kicked-started many of the insecurities, anger issues, and resentments in my life.

Both of my parents worked, so my sisters and I would stay over at my cousins oftentimes and get picked up later in the day when one of them would get off. As time went on, those nights got longer, and the reason for this is that there was a rift that occurred between my parents.

My father was involved in an affair that was beginning to destroy my family. By no means was my father a bad man. In fact, we were actually close during my younger years and spent a lot of time with each other, but his acts of infidelity was beginning to take its effect on my mother's ability to continue to breathe life into something that was dying. I can't really blame my father, he did what he knew. His father was a "rolling stone" and he didn't break the generational curse so he fell to it also. He perpetuated what he saw as a kid. When she gave up her will to stop trying, she also fell into the realms of an adulterous relationship. The constant arguments and fighting became customary in the Collins household. Though my mother was wrong to indulge in her relationship outside the marriage, the resentment strongly surfaced with my father. I always thought if he could have just focused on the big picture of his family, the walls of that house wouldn't have experienced the things that it did. Around this time my mother was also pregnant with my brother Jeremy. With all the changes and stress of the marriage, she had him early, and he passed shortly after birth. When the news finally hit me, I became the angry delinquent child whom no one wanted to deal with.

Soon after, my parents separated, and both went their separate ways with my sisters and I living with my mother. After the separation, I saw very little of my father, and after a while I grew numb to him even being around. I became very protective of my mother and ultimately a "mama's boy."

By the time, it was all said and done, I had harness so much resentment and anger toward my father that it was hard to ever believe anything he would say and our close relationship was far gone by the time I was ten years old.

It was really tough for my mother. I would see her trying to work two and three jobs to make sure we had good Christmases and back-to-school items. My sisters would get the first of everything, and though it was not meant for me to be overlooked, it felt that way. I would have to wear clothes that were too small and old just so my sisters could have everything they needed until my time came.

I would hate having to walk to school with my friends, and they had all the latest apparel, and I would have to make up some excuse why I could not wear my "new stuff" yet. Coupled with the fact that every school that I attended in my youth, I was the darkest kid at the school, so I got made fun of often. I hated my skin color growing up and envied the fair-skinned kids.

Every "so black" joke created, I heard throughout the course of my life. Even if I had a crush on a girl and she liked me back at the grade school and middle school age, she would not admit it because of the risk of being ridiculed for liking the dark kid. This kind of treatment happened to me up through my sophomore year in high school. I never expressed the hurt that it caused me because I always felt the best way to deal with my internal issues were not to talk about them, which initiated my trust issues.

I could never tell who my real friends were because if the popular kids teased me, the friends I did have usually migrated toward them eventually. Ninety percent of the time in my life, even as I write my story, I felt alone, insecure, and abandoned. Spending so much time alone, I developed a large mental capacity for imagination and fantasy. I would imagine myself doing great things, having a beautiful wife, and living the American dream.

As I got older, I began to write many of my thoughts down on paper in the form of poems. It was really the only way I could express things that I would not be unable to say. For the most part, I believe writing and my broad imagination kept me sane.

My mother and father were both Christians and had a background of attending and being involved in church. My mother understood the importance of spirituality and always made us go to church. The church we grew up in was still located down the street from my grandparent's home in Los Angeles. In fact, it was the "family church."

My mother and her siblings were raised in this church, and mostly all of my cousins were raised in this church. Usually on Sundays, we would go to church and after go over to my grandparents where we spent a lot of our Sunday nights sitting in the back room until it was time to leave. I loved Sundays because it was a time the family got together to eat and just have a good time until we all went our separate ways that evening. For me that time meant a lot more to me than probably everyone else because when I got home, I went back into my shell.

My sisters had all their friends and for the most part played together, but me, I just had my own thoughts and illusions. As I grew and matured, I found it hard to deal with my personal issues in a positive manner. The temper that I developed as a child was becoming harder to suppress overtime, and I would have moments where I would lash out at the wrong times.

I would hate when my mother would slap us with another "we're moving" speech. It became evident to me as I was growing that we were not moving because Mom was getting a new job or that we were moving into bigger better places to live but because things would get overwhelming for my mother and we would move because we were either getting evicted or unable to continue to pay rent at that particular location. In my childhood, I can remember my sisters and I lived in nine different places within a twelve-year period. It was not until 1998 when my family began to find some true stability.

My mother had remarried, and we moved over into a mobile home park into a double wide mobile home in Ontario, California. Even though my mother had remarried, I was still very protective of her. It took me a little time to get used to my stepfather being the man of the house because I was afraid he might take my mother through another dramatic phase in her life.

There was actually a time my stepfather and I got into a physical altercation because there was a felt battle of who was the dominant male figure in the home. I had too much pride to let my stepfather be the man of the house. People tried to tell me that I could not let him be that dominant figure because I was jealous of him and my mom's relationship, but as I grew older and have a better understanding of things, I do not believe that was the case at all. I wanted my mother to be happy and be with a man who would love and cherish her like she deserved, so I would not have been jealous of that. I understand now, and through the research that I have done, I concluded that the real reason I could not then was that I did not trust that he could do the job.

For me trust had to be earned, and I was not giving him the chance, but as time passed, I saw the genuine man in him and was able to give that respect and trust over to him that he deserved and should have received from the time he stepped into our lives.

Now my father also remarried. In fact, he actually married a few years before my mother did, and though formally he and my mother were not together technically, they still were married when he began dating his current wife. In all honesty, I actually talk more kindly to my stepmother than to my stepfather. I truly believe the reason for this is that with my stepmother, she was able to give me what I longed for, and that was a brother.

Between both of my blended families, I have three brothers and a total of five sisters. I never really saw any of my blended siblings in the "step" form. I cared for them as if they were my own blood siblings.

Though I had many issues, I always had a heart to care for people. Part of my downfall later in my story came from the feeling of caring too much for people and them continuing to let me down. It really got to the point where I told myself that I was going to do to them what they did to me. If I had let someone down, I really didn't feel much pain behind it. My only goal was to be the best person I could be and do my best to eventually take care of my family. So during the times my dad was around, I did not have many issues going over with them and spending time with my stepmother and her children. I give her a lot of credit because she really tried to make us comfortable when we were around.

There were times I pretended like I did not like being around her, but I really did. Basically I did it out of respect for my mother and her feelings toward the situation with my father's new lady. I owed it to her to at least fake my resentment toward my stepmother sometimes. Those visits diminished when my father took his family six hours away to Sacramento, California. From then on, that part of my family was out of sight, out of mind to me.

A Loose Canon and Puppy Love

Like I mentioned before, this was around the time we kind of had settled in one area, and for the most part my middle school years were up and down emotionally but for the most part fairly smooth despite the ridicule of my skin color that I was at this point accustomed to.

Middle school was where I really began to test the waters of talking and entertaining girls. To the best of my knowledge, I got shut down more times that I could remember. It's because in fact every girl I wanted to be my girlfriend shut me down and shut me down hard. Not one girl wanted to talk to me. The insecurity continued to mount, and eventually, if I did not find an outlet, my temper that I developed would have taken form in a very different way that may not have me alive today. I would go home so angry because I did not know how to handle rejection, and ultimately it led to me picking up athletics. I had always been a natural athlete, so to get into extracurricular activities, I chose to get into track-and-field along with basketball.

Though I was better at track-and-field, basketball is what carried me into my high school and college years and what I become accustomed to participating in 24/7. Yet even in sports, it was hard for me to handle disappointment. When I first began playing organized ball, I wasn't very good, and I sat the bench a lot. I knew I was a decent player, but my middle school coach thought otherwise. It was in middle school where I truly embraced being a loner. Even when I stayed in and my mother was around, I got to the point where I did not even want to be around her like I used to with her being married and all.

I had my own room, so I stayed to myself there until it was time to eat, but even then, I made my plate and went to back to my room to eat. My family never ate at the table together. I found a special love for music and poetry, and I began to write thoughts and different ideas down on paper that I was feeling. Poetry was a way for me to express stuff that I would not normally be able to speak out loud. Even as a minister now, I cannot show some of the poetry that I have written because it may be too explicit in regards to the position that I'm in now. I have even played with the idea of putting my poetry in book form because I have some pretty powerful ones, but I may revisit that later on at another period in my life.

The friends that I did try to have in middle school didn't seem to have my best interest at heart. I got introduced to things that I shouldn't have. Because of my firm foundation from my mother, there were times where I did not indulge in the peer pressure, but it was through these relationships that I had my first intoxicating beverage, pornography experience, and developed a filthy mouth.

Now though, I was introduced to these things I had not yet built a proclivity for, so at this point in my life, they were easy to let go of. I had never masturbated, so I really did not understand the purpose of porn, and I did not like smoking or drugs all that much, so I always found an excuse to avoid using them. I just wanted to be so much like these kids my age who had no curfew, guidance, or sense of stability that I begin to do the things that they did. The ironic thing was the friends who were positive influences were the ones I mistreated because the friends I was trying to be like mistreated them. I can remember one friend who would give me rides to school every now and again, and we used to walk home together every day, but he was an easy target for being picked on because he never wanted to fight or stick up for himself. So I guess he was friends with me the same reason I was friends with my bad influences.

I did have another really positive friend whom I spent most of my days walking home from school with, and I think the reason was because I had a major crush on her, and just the mere fact that she entertained me was satisfying enough. This young lady and I spent hours on the phone and had hundreds of conversations about everything and nothing at the same time. So when I thought I was doing well, it broke my heart when she called me and said those words that no guy wants to hear when he likes a particular girl and decides to express his feelings to her: "I like you but as a friend." I think that was my last plea for trying to have a girlfriend in middle school. That was about two years of hard work and conversations to no avail. Yet, to this day this woman and I are still good friends and still talk from time to time.

In middle school is where I met one of my closest friends to date; yet we didn't know that we would cross paths to the degree that we did. The last year of middle school, I decided to play flag football for my team. We had played a team from another part of the city. On this other team was a kid by the name of James. I didn't understand why, but this kid just kept talking trash to me. I wasn't even a football player, but he must have been intimidated because he wouldn't shut up (though his story tells it a different way I'm sure). Well it turns out that James and I ended up at the same high school, and the moment I saw him I knew exactly who he was, "that kid that would not shut up." I guess you can say I kind of took it personally that he didn't know me but felt the need to continually speak on my athletic ability during that flag football game. Yet James becomes pivotal in my story because I did not know that this trash-talking kid would serve as an important figure in my life and become one of my closest friends later in life.

During middle school, even with athletics serving as an outlet for my bad temper, I not only was at odds with my stepfather, but I also found myself getting into physical altercations at school. I knew if I fought at school, my mother would hear about it, so I would usually meet to fight someone away from the school grounds. I wasn't afraid to fight even if that meant with my own family. If I felt threatened in any kind of way, I would lash out, I even found myself doing it at basketball and track practice when a teammate would come at me in a way I didn't feel was appropriate. The closer I got to high school, the more I learned to harness and suppress my temper. As I was transitioning to high school, my maturity started developing and eventually was able to see that fighting would ultimately continue to land me in situations I didn't want to be in. The more enemies I kept creating meant the more people who would continue to try to take me out.

The Loner Meets His Bestest

High school took its toll on me emotionally and mentally. I still remained a loner for most of my high school years. A lot of this had to do with me going to another school where I had friends different from all my peers in middle school. My oldest sister had issues at the local school that we were supposed to attend based on our address, so my mother decided that it was best for us to attend the school that was out of our district. It was significantly out of the way so much that my siblings and I had to take the city bus to attend school. I was pretty infuriated when this happened because I generally only had two or three faithful friends who were really close to me throughout middle school, so when I separated from them, it was hard for me to handle.

For a kid who kept to himself most of the time, to have his only few companions forced away from him coupled with the fact that he suffered from extreme insecurity issues and the only people who cared enough to entertain him were those few individuals was great joy for him. As I mentioned earlier, the young lady whom I grew fond of was going to a different school than I, and though she had made it clear that she had no interest in me, I was certain I could change her mind as time passed, and we got older, unfortunately this was not going to happen.

My first few months in high school, if you are following my story, you can probably guess that I was a loner. I did know a few girls who ended up at the same high school as I, but they had a different lunch period, so that opportunity to hang out with them quickly evaporated. For months, I sat off into the quad (a large place in the middle of campus where students hung out for lunch) during my lunch breaks and time in between classes before the second bell rang. My older sister Latoya has always been able to attract attention. She was a young beautiful brown-skinned attractive girl who was just always able to fit in with the in crowd. Most brothers in my position would easily find a way in the inner circle when their sister is in one but not me. I did not want to be in the shadow of my sister.

A Preacher's Struggle

If I had to relate my sister's relationship with me to a relevant famous family, it would be that of the R&B singer Brandy and her little brother Ray J. No matter how much Ray J tried (even going as far as making an adult home video), he was always in the shadow of his sister's fame. Because my sister had the "it" factor when it came to being one of the popular kids, no matter what I did, I was always going to be referred to as "Oh, that's Toya's little brother." With that being my motivation to have independence away from my sister, I remained invisible to many people.

My freshman year in high school was really nothing to remember. I couldn't wait for school to end, so I could get home to my place of peace, my solitude, my comfort zone. I attempted to play basketball, but after being cut from the team because I allowed my grades to drop significantly from middle school, it left me with no outlet. I reverted my anger back to my father and his lack of follow through. When people would say things I didn't like, I would snap (even to those in my family).

I remember a close female cousin of mine and I had gotten into it at her house, and the altercation got physical because I did not know how to control my emotions. In fact, this kin in particular and I had a number of altercations. I believe the reason for this was that she was the female version of me. We both would harvest anger from past issues that on the right day with the right negative comment, we would explode.

I remember vividly that during a family reunion vacation, we were at Disneyland, and we had gotten into an argument so heavy that I called her a "B" (word I don't use anymore, but I'm sure you figured it out) in front of all these people, and she slapped half the black off my face. I mean for a moment, I felt like the Prophet Jeremiah when she hit me. It was like fire shut up in my face! Man that hurt. Now though I had no filter and regard for authority, I knew better than to put my hands on her to the degree that she did to me especially not in a public area with a lot of children around. It took another one of my cousins to pull me away from the situation to calm me down. Through the years, this individual and I have grown really close. We would ride together, have deep conversations, and share many laughs with one another (even about the crazy arguments we had).

Freshman year faded, and the summer came and went. Sophomore year of high school was approaching, and it was October of my sophomore year that everything changed. In fact, it took a turn for the better, which in turn led to the worst turn of my life. It was a man by the name of Sam High, the junior varsity basketball coach, who canopied me into the kid known as Lou and not Toya's little brother any longer.

Early in my sophomore year of high school, I met a few friends. Through sitting in classes and finding certain things in common with other peers, I found myself associating with various people. I still always had a proclivity to play basketball and was fairly talented at it. Even though I had this talent, I was still not convinced that I should play as an extracurricular activity. Coach High was the junior varsity basketball coach and approached me one day about playing. I was resistant still, but my friend Matt always seemed to have a way of pulling me into things with him because he made them sound so appealing. So I went out for the team and during the tryout process and first few practices, I shined. For a player to be fairly out of shape and had not played in a little bit over a year, my natural talent propelled me to one of the better players on the team.

Most of the guys on the team were pretty popular in their own right. They were the type of guys who had all the latest clothes, shoes, and always had money. I felt like somebody being around these guys, and though I didn't have even close to what many of these guys had, they still accepted me as one of them. Many times, I felt that they pitied me because I did not have much. I was now part of the in crowd, and the dynamics of my personality became more confident in correlation with who I was associated with.

I soon adopted a nickname my teammates gave me, "Lou," and still today, it has stuck as I moved through every transition of my life. Even with my new band of associates, I was still a church boy to a degree. One thing that my mother never wavered in was keeping our family in church. It did not matter when I had a game or how late that game lasted. I would always be in church when church was going on. This was a point in my life where I actually felt good about myself, so I became pretty involved in my church. I was about fifteen years old when I decided that I wanted to be more involved in church functions and activities. I began to sing in my church choir, participate more in youth church, and even joined our praise dancing team at church where I was one of two males in a sea of women. My family was still struggling, but for the first time in my life, I felt a sense of security in my life and about who I was. Yet it did not last very long.

When the season began and our JV team began to play games, I found myself at the end of the bench. Now I know for a fact that I was one of the more talented players on the roster. Even players who were in the starting five would approach me and feel bad because some of them felt I should be playing over them. I did not understand why I was not playing. It became apparent to me that though Coach High was a good guy, he had his favorites. Coach High was also a proctor (security) at the high school that I attended, and he had great relationships with those who had played for him the year before off the court also.

Outside of basketball practice, Coach and I never really spoke. I was unsure how to handle the situation, so I did not say anything. I continued to watch games from the bench and cry once I got off the school bus that we traveled on. Once again, I felt rejected. I would give my all in practice, work as hard as I could, but it went unnoticed. It was the game that we played our crosstown rivals, Ontario High School (the school I was supposed to attend), and saw all my friends from middle school that I played with where I made a decision in my life that still today I live by, and that is to make people remember me. During the final game of my first year of playing ball, I was so infuriated it pushed me into a mentality that I do not and will never regret for the rest of my life. The night that I was in front of my old friends and I did not play one second of that game is when I became a go-getter. I was never again going to allow anyone to control what I could or could not have, and that night, the beast was unleashed in me.

During that second year of high school, I met a girl, and I grew really fond of her. She was very attractive, and I loved everything about her. Jay and I grew incredibly close as friends. Even though I pursued her as a love interest first, I found myself intrigued by her friendship. She made me feel like somebody. She stroked my ego to the point that I thought I was the only guy that mattered in her life. This was far from the truth. In my story, there are only three women who I can honestly say that I would have dropped everything just to be with them starting with my bestest.

With my sister graduated and I having somewhat of a name in the in-crowd, I was beginning to establish some type of identity about myself. Much happened over the course of that summer before school started. I had become the face of the praise dancing team that I was a part of. I began to attend a more local youth group on Wednesday nights where I connected with peers from other schools, Jay's friendship with me had gone to another level, I had experienced my first real girlfriend (lasted about three months), and my mother became more open to me staying out late and over friends' houses. The apex of this time period in my life is that for some odd reason out of nowhere, dark-skinned guys had taken over and was getting all the play from girls. I like to think that a few dark-skinned celebrities helped save the dark brothers because for a while, we were struggling to get conversation. With that said, it was my junior year that the ugly duckling appearance began to morph. I was making my own money by doing little side jobs with my aunt and saving a little money that I was able to buy things that I wanted. I was dressing and keeping myself together a lot better than my first two years of high school. I was buying name branded shoes and clothes that also got me a fair share of attention.

The relationship that Jay and I had was tighter than any relationship I had at this time in my life. We were so close that even when she was having issues in her home, she would call me first. We would buy each other gifts for every holiday there is. We had met early in the year of my second year in high school, and by the time school started, in my junior year, we were looking for each other on the first day of class. Now Jay had also come into her shape and attractiveness. Guys have always seen her as cute, but by her junior year, she went from being a cute girl to a bad chick whom guys wanted to get at. Much of her attractiveness was because she was built very nicely. Jay ran track, and track girl bodies were the best. To some degree, they still are. After all the conversations and building our friendship, I thought it was time that I seriously decided to move in and claim what was mine once and for all. Writing letters were how we used to communicate if we liked someone. We would make all these different shapes that we would fold the letter into and more.

Writing letters to Jay was not an uncommon thing we did. We wrote notes all the time and gave them to each other in between class periods, but this time, I decided I was going to tell Jay how I felt about her and ask her if she wanted to be more than friends. Her reply letter expressed that though we were close friends she was not sure if she liked me in that way. She mentioned that I was attractive to her, and she would date me, but that she did not want a boyfriend. I was alright with the answer she gave me because in my mind, based on her reply, I at least had a chance in the future. I was feeling pretty decent about myself because I knew I was going to get her just not right now. That all quickly changed because I hit a low at the beginning of my junior year when I found out that Jay started dating a guy a week after I wrote her that letter. I was hurt. When one of my fellow teammates told me, I did not know how to respond. I was screaming on the inside but acted like I didn't care on the outside. When I saw her after I found out, we both made eye contact, and we both knew that this would change the dynamics of our friendship. I, being the person that I am, accepted it and continued to be there when she needed me. It got to the point where I felt uncomfortable at times when we would write notes to each other and talk on the phone because at some point, the conversation would shift to her boyfriend and their issues.

I stayed good friends with Jay while I pursued other girls in high school. As much as I tried, I just could not get over how much I felt about her. Now as time passed, my focus shifted to basketball. I had worked so hard that previous summer because I never wanted to sit on the bench again that I worked my way into the starting five of the varsity team in my junior year. With me being a starter and significant player on my team, my popularity continued to grow. Even with the growth of my own individuality, the only thing I really wanted was Jay. Watching her date guys who didn't treat her right and at the same time continuously turn the one good guy that had her best interest at heart down became taxing on me emotionally. I would go home and ask myself, "What's wrong with me? Why can't she see me? What do these other guys have that I don't?" Even though I was young, I had adult type relationship feelings for Jay.

I would constantly ask her why she looks past me, and she could never really give me an answer, but I continued to have hope that one day she could see me for what I was trying to be to her. So I just continued to support her relationships apart from me, and when she needed my advice on something, I was there to lend it to her. Things came full surface when she had a relationship with a guy whom she knew I did not like. I hated this guy. I did not like his persona nor how I've heard he treated some of his friends in the past. I knew he was not good for her, but she decided that's who she wanted to be with, and things came to a climax when he began to treat her wrong, and it resulted to full-fledged fireworks between me and my entourage and this guy and his.

If it was not for Jay herself, there would have been a brawl, or even riot the way my boys rolled. It was so bad I had friends from surrounding schools on call to come up to my school if things would have popped off. Even with all that, Jay could not see that I loved her and would do anything to protect her. Or maybe she saw it but did not want to be with me, and I would have been all right with that if I had known that. I was young, so my optimism was at an all-time high, coupled with the pledge that I made to myself that I would never give up on something that I wanted.

It was the common sense of a friend that I had become close with and was also teammates with that made me think about the bigger picture of the issue. You know him as the kid I referred to as talking too much during a flag football game, but I know him as "Jroc" James. James and I had grown fond of each other over the years in school. When I learned more about him as a person, we became real cool friends. We were teammates on the basketball court as well. James was always a levelheaded person. In his young age, he knew how to put situations in their proper perspective. During my up and downs with Jay, I would talk to James about how I felt about her, and he would keep me encouraged and always told me, "Don't sweat that, Lou."

James was always there for me when I needed to talk or just to vent to someone. Even today, he is still a great outlet where I can get some things off my chest. It is even more insightful now because in our conversations, we actually talk about God because we both have come into our own spirituality. Over time, Jay and I did finally have a period in which we decided to date, but after all that I had been through with her coupled with me having trust issues based on prior relationship, there was no way to sustain what we had, so you can say it ended almost as fast as it began.

I was committed to being there for Jay, and as we became adults, time and distance took us away from each other. I still reach back every now and then and shoot her a text just to see if she is doing all right. She is doing well and has her own little family that she looks after. A month after meeting her, I vowed I would be her "bestest." It was an inside commitment that I would stand by her no matter what, and that I did.

Sold Out,
the Church Boy Experience

As mentioned earlier, I came from a family that was solid Christians. Even though the church that I had grown up in did not teach holiness to the extent that I understand it today, I still had a solid grasp on what was right and wrong.

I was always involved at some level with my church, and toward the beginning of my senior year in high school, my extracurricular activities for the most part revolved around the church. With my infatuation on Jay slowly diminishing and really seeing no reason to engage in some of the things my teammates were doing because they were not appealing to me, I looked to my church.

Now around this time, I had been involved with a group of praise dancers at my home church, and we were known all over the city of Los Angeles. When I say *known*, I mean we were always the talk in the church sector when it came to being invited to various church events. We were known as "God's Praise Dancers." The name was given to us by the late pastor of my home church. We would literally shut churches down that after we had finished, ministering the whole service would have been shifted to pure worship. With me being the only male in the group for some time now, I had become the face of the group and led many of the dances.

When we would get done, I would hear so much about how much of an inspiration I was to the group and a gift that I had to minister through dance. This was the first time I realized that I had a special anointing to do ministry. I knew something was on my life, but I could not pinpoint exactly what it was. As time went on, I would lead songs in the choir, be the leader of certain auxiliaries, and eventually will be a keynote speaker for our small youth services that we would have. After a while, I began to get this feeling that what I was doing at my home church was not enough for me. Our youth was not that big in membership, and I have become of age to understand that the church's business meetings were more about getting rid of a pastor rather than taking care of actual business.

I began to see that there were issues with the leadership of that church and that it was not a church conducive to my spiritual growth. I had asked the question what happened to these people. Now at this time, we lived about forty-five minutes away from my church and would have to commute quite a ways to attend every Sunday. Not too long after I got invited from a good friend to attend his church youth camp did I start attending his church. The church was a lot closer to the area that I lived. Needless to say when I went to this camp, immediately I knew that this would be my new home on Wednesdays for youth group and some Sundays when my mother permitted me to attend. I mean everything I could ask in a youth group this church had. It was young, innovative, had cute girls, large in size, had cute girls, relatable, had cute girls, great youth leaders, and had many more cute girls!

I instantly fell in love with this church and the youth group that I went to the youth leader and asked how I can be a part of this group permanently. He simply said, "Just keep showing up." It is through this youth group that I found by far one of my closest friends I have today.

Lindy, as I know her, would become my rock later on in my life as she was an intricate part in my corner because she always gave me hope. Within a month of being a part of that church, I started going to church services and youth group activities and services that the church hosted. I had become accustomed to a group of young people who were sold out about serving God. I even took my gift that I had with my home church and planted it in my new ministry where I was serving when a beautiful woman, who was the youth pastor's wife, approached a group of us young men about a male praise dance group. She had not known that I was and had been a part of a dance group at my previous church, so when she asked me, I was more than willing to participate.

The "young men of God" group dynamics were different from that of the God's praise dancers in that with God's praise dancers, we told stories through our ministry by using the song that was playing. Young men of God were more of contemporary movements to gospel ballets. However, both groups were effective in their own way. As our popularity grew, the Young Men of God began to get invites to dance at other's church events around the community. Even as I look back at that time in my life things were good, I had a voice among young people, I was well respected by my peers outside of just my athletic talents, and people liked me. I really felt like I was somebody. I felt so good about how things were going in my life that it carried over into my everyday life at school.

I would start bringing my Bible to school and going off to myself to read it. I had stopped cussing and trying to chase a bunch of girls. Notice I said "a bunch," which means my count went down a little bit, but not all the way. I loved the ladies and was known as one of the top flirts at the school. Yet, even in my conversations with them, I ask them if they went to a church, if they believe in God, and if they wanted to come to my youth group. For the first time, I was actually learning stuff about the Bible that I've never known. Even the stories I did grow up hearing were presented to me in a new exciting way that made me excited to go and study more. Though I was still loyal to my home church and the activities I was involved in that church was no longer being attributed to me as my church, if I went, it was because I had a responsibility to the praise dancers or my mother made me go because she wanted me to come to church with her.

In her mind, I believe she knew the church I grew up in was no longer my home and my mother had matured to a point in her own faith that she was all right with that. Many people get stuck in the "family church" because it's all they have known throughout generations, but I had found somewhere that suited me, that I enjoyed, and that's all I believe my mother wanted.

My senior year was flourishing in all areas of my life. Spiritually I felt whole, socially I felt like I was a part of something great, academically I was doing well and had begun to apply for colleges, and athletically I had become the most polarized player on my basketball team by being in the paper week after week. I had developed a heart for people and a heart for ministry that reached beyond the walls of a church. I would try to reach out to individuals who would be involved in things that were antithetical to the Word of God.

I would see much of my old self in many young men, the cussing, the smoking, the drinking, and all of it just to fit into a crowd. I hated to see people hurting and struggling because I knew what it felt like. When a person would start crying because of what they were going through, I would cry with them because in some weird way I would feel what they were feeling, and for the most part, things were going decently in my life. I was ministry, I was sold out. With life going so well I thought they couldn't get any better. I was wrong. There was this really attractive girl that I had been into sometime at the youth ministry I was serving in. She actually attended my rival school, but as we began to talk and get to know each other, I found myself hanging out with her on her campus after school more than mine. We immediately clicked, and I thought she was the hottest thing smoking!

I asked her to my senior prom, and without hesitation, she quickly replied, "Of course, I will go with you." In fact I actually fasted for a whole day that she would say yes when I asked her. Prom night was one of the most memorable nights for me. My mother went out of her way to get me a limo, my grandfather took me to downtown Los Angeles to pick me out a fresh three-piece baby blue and silver suit (don't hate. That mug was too fresh), and I had the finest caramel-looking girl on my arm. I told myself this was the life. God was really being good to me.

The night went so well that by the time we left to go home, this young lady was officially my girlfriend. I remember when we got to her house we sat in the limo and just talked for a while. Then we kissed and talk and then kissed some more. I had even entertained the idea of losing my virginity to her that night in the back of the limo, but God kept us. From that night on, my girl and I were tight. We had a bond so strong that I literally thought I would have the famous love story of marrying my high school sweetheart. Unfortunately, things didn't turn out like that and took a turn for the worst.

I was approaching the end of my high school career when I had gotten an invite to visit a college in the small town of McPherson, Kansas. The school was a NAIA (National Associations of Intercollegiate Athletics) school athletically. I knew I wanted to play ball in college but just wasn't sure where yet, in fact I was actually better at track and field and had two NCAA partial scholarship offers, but I was burnt out from track and decided I did not want to run anymore. I visited this school with my uncle, and to be honest, my visit wasn't that great. My host locked me out the room for hours, I did not enjoy the food, and the town seemed so boring. Nevertheless, I felt a sense that I belonged there.

It was a Christian college, and with all that I had been doing back home, it just felt like the right place to get away and become my own man. Little did I know that making this decision in my life would take me on a roller coaster that almost lead me to taking my own life but ultimately pushed me into my purpose. So before I left, I signed my letter of intent to play basketball there and headed back home. When I got back home, things had become weird between me and my girlfriend. It was like she was uninterested in anything I had to say anymore, and we just began to argue. Even the vibe that I felt when I would come to the youth group and talk with some of her friends was uncomfortable, as if they knew something that I didn't. My girlfriend then called me one day and informed me that she doesn't want to date anymore. This came as a surprise because though we were still having our rough moments, we were equally having our good ones as well.

I asked her why, and she said that it was because I am leaving, and we will be so far away from each other. This was interesting to me because we had already had plenty of conversations about how we were going to stick it out and stay together because my plan was to try it out for a year, and if I was unhappy, I would move back or closer to home. However, I honored her wish to break up because I had a feeling that I would get back with her eventually.

A week or so passed, and I saw her, and she didn't say anything to me. We were still planning on being friends, but she had just stopped talking to me. Slowly information began to surface about another guy, who happened to be her ex, and how they had started talking again. I initially had no problem with it because we were broken up but the timing of her dating again was pretty quick. The problem that I had and I still have is that I love hard. If I say I love you, it is unconditional. My heart is so big that I want to see people do well and have all that they desire. I'm so loyal to people that when they are not loyal back or my loyalty gets rejected, it does something to me that emotionally diminishes me. I eventually caught wind from mutual friends that she was talking and seeing this guy while we were still in our relationship. That ate me up on the inside. I was hurt.

The pain surfaced so much that I exploded during a youth night. I went off on every person who knew about it. The old short-tempered Lou made an appearance after being on a hiatus for a long while. It was hard for me to handle because I had put all my eggs in this basket for this young lady. After being comforted by a few friends, I made a public announcement in youth group Bible study about how my behavior was inappropriate and that it would never happen again., and it wouldn't because I told myself that night once I got home that I would not be rejected again, I would not hurt again, and I would not allow myself to be the victim of emotional abuse again. I made a vow that from then on, I was going to do to women what they have done to me my whole life. Little did I know that having that mind-set opened the door to a curse that has plagued the men on my father's side of the family. Even though I was still a virgin at the time that night without me recognizing it, I birthed my addition to sex.

My First Time

With the embarrassment of all that had happened with my ex-girlfriend, my attendance at that youth group slowly depleted. I started going back to my home church that I grew up in a lot more than usual and killed time until I was to move to Kansas. Jay, Lindy, and my good friend Brandon had been a support system for me through all that I had gone through in that short period of time. They were really the only three individuals I would have conversations with about anything that had to do with personal issues in my life. They have always been in my corner rooting for me. Before I knew it, I was graduating from high school, made a little money over the summer, and was heading east to McPherson. I didn't look back.

As I arrived on campus, I had this weird feeling, as if I was out of place. Immediately, I wanted to head back to California. Yet, when orientation started, I began to feel more comfortable around the people there. My roommate was a really cool guy, and as a few days went on with hanging around my teammates and getting to know some really cool professors, my homesickness ultimately evaporated. I had always been a pretty decent student academically, but I lost focus when I started college. I had become focused on being the cool guy and going out with friends that it took my eyes off what I was in Kansas for.

I had started staying out partying, clubbing, drinking, and smoking on a consistent basis. I had experienced with it earlier in life but not to the extent that I was now indulging. One night, while hanging out in my dorm room with a few of my teammates, I had made the mistake of telling them that I was still a virgin. We had been talking about sexual acts and all the things that we had done with women, and I was the only one in the room that had not experienced sexual intercourse. I had been with women in other sexual ways but never in the most intimate of them all. Initially, when I expressed that I was a virgin, I thought the response would be more welcoming because it would be seen as a good thing. I always knew it was respectable, but it was the

A Preacher's Struggle

idea of just being able to say that I've done it seemed more appealing to me.

When I left that conversation, it seemed like water under the bridge for everyone else, but for me it kept resonating in my mind about how I was a virgin and the curiosity about sex. With the curiosity being so heavy, I told myself that at the first opportunity, I was going to experience sex. All the talks about abstinence and saving myself until marriage went out the window. I no longer cared about saving myself. I told myself that it was time to be the type of person that society expected me to be, and with my history of women and heartbreak, I felt that every woman I got involved with had it coming. I decided to go to the club one night. Generally, I don't believe in finding a "girlfriend" at the club, but I do believe it is definitely the spot for a "hookup." I had one thing on my mind and one thing only, to find a woman and have sex with her.

I met a young lady who had interest in me, and for some reason, it felt like she had the same goals as I did. We started talking and exchanged numbers. Now this woman seemed like a very nice girl and could be someone to have a potential relationship with, but that was the last thing on my mind. I met her on a Thursday night, and we talked for two days, and on Saturday night, it happened in the back of a SUV. I lost my virginity.

I barely knew this woman; in fact I really knew nothing about her. Till this day, all I remember is her name and not even her last name. I finally knew what sex felt like. I, being so proud of myself, quickly ran back to the dorm to tell one of my teammates, and his response rocked me to the core, and I will never forget it. The first words that came out of his mouth was "What you do that for, Lou?" It shook me so much that feelings of rage came over me. He expressed that just because the guys had a conversation about it and you were the only virgin does not mean that you should go do something as dumb as sleep with any girl your first time. He continued on to express how they had lost their virginity to girls they had been with for a long time or friends that they knew for a while. I had no words, and the only encouraging thing he had to say was "Whelp, you are part of the club now!"

I left that conversation feeling like complete dirt. I was infuriated at myself. I didn't want to be bothered by anyone. I took a long walk around the small town, angry at myself for the decision that I made and couldn't get back. It angered me so much that it sent my mind into a place that I felt if I was going to be this angry at myself, I was going to find an outlet, and my new outlet for aggression was going to be sex. The issues that I thought I had a handle on surfaced back up: my temper, insecurities, and not feeling good enough for anybody. I felt rejected again because I did not receive the welcoming response that I thought I would for losing my virginity. So for the lack of a better statement, I built up a clientele within a week of women that I could call for sex.

Within two weeks of losing my virginity, I had had sexual intercourse with three different women multiple times. One of the women of the three wanted a relationship with me, and when she told me, I slept with her and never called back again. Until this day, the last conversation I had with her was "See you later. Hit me up sometime," but that was the last time we ever saw or talked to each other because I never returned a call.

My mind would not let me get to the point where my emotions felt bad about anything. At the risk of bragging about something I'm not proud of, I got so good at the game that I would see multiple girls that I slept with at the club who all went to the same school and neither of them knew that I was sleeping with all of them on a regular basis. I created a "don't ask, don't tell" rule for myself. If they asked whether I was messing with another girl, I told them the truth, and whatever they thought of me afterward was completely up to them. If they didn't ask, then they were out of sight, out of mind. If I was with that particular girl that night, she had my attention. If it wasn't her night, she never got a phone call, text message, email or any other form of communication until I felt like it.

At this point in my life, I had no filter. I was getting drunk on a regular basis, indulged in smoking occasionally, and if you had a problem with me, my hands were not only good with women but pretty gully in a fight also. I always tell people, if I'm honest with myself, boxing was really my first sport. I enjoyed fighting people when I was younger. My life had taken a turn for the worst, but the ironic and, to a degree, sad part about it is that I was loving every moment of it. I became "the man" in college. There was a core group of us that people knew were the "get-it-in crew." They knew if we were all together, we were not doing volunteer community service work, and it didn't take much for us to "turn up" at a party or night club.

My freshman year in college, a friend, and teammate, and I created what we called "I don't give a crap" week (except *crap* wasn't the word we used back then). It usually was the week before finals, and there were no rules. We went to class drunk and high. I remember taking a lemonade bottle and filling it up with McCormick Vodka (hey, give me a break I was in college and couldn't afford the expensive stuff yet) and was drinking in class because vodka has a really light smell to it to the point where a person can't really smell it at all when mixed with juice.

My friend was getting plastered in the dorm room before class, and during that whole week, we had all kinds of women in and out of our rooms. I remind you that this is a Christian college, and for the most part, the rules were significantly strict, we just made up in our minds that we were going to disregard everything the school was about and live how we wanted. It was during this week that we had gone to the club, and I had gotten invited to go to a girl's house, a girl whom I've been trying to get with all semester that went to our rival college across town. She just kept shutting me down, and I was really trying to get with her. She invited me over to her house, and it was then that she told me that she is a lesbian. I'm shocked. I said to myself, "Okay, why am I here?" but her girlfriend had always wanted to have a guy in the bed with them (they both had been with men before), and because of the risk of degrading women and the fact that I don't agree or celebrate what took place next, I will omit the rest of that story.

I felt like I couldn't be touched, that this is the way I should have been living my whole life. At this stage in my life, I didn't understand why anyone would want to be a virgin. When school had let out, I returned home, and it was clear to my mother that something was different about me. I wanted to stay out with my friends all night, and when my mother had picked me up from a friend's house, she could tell I had been drinking. I was not drunk, but she could smell it. My mother and I had always had an open relationship, and I didn't keep things from her, so before she could ask, I spoke with her about some of the things that I was doing and that I just wanted to live my life and that I didn't feel like I was hurting anyone. She had her concerns, but ultimately she had come to grips while I was away that I was my own man, and the decisions that I was making were mine to make.

She didn't get into a tug-of-war match or argument with me but told me to be careful and remember that God sees all. I heard her, but I was enjoying the lifestyle too much to heed to the advice. The best thing my mother did that day was put me in God's hands and took hers off me. She understood that life had its own consequences, and she would not be able to save me from them with how I was living, yet at the same time she was confident with how she raised me.

California is known for beautiful women all the time, so I was like a kid in a candy shop. I could not bring them home because that first summer back, I stayed with my mother. I would go over to friends' apartments who had their own places and do my dirt there. I also began to surprise myself with the type of women I was sleeping with. I had no conscience. There was this woman who was extremely beautiful. She was actually aspiring to be a swimsuit model. I had been with pretty women before but not like this. Everything about this woman was in a man's dream girl, she was of Egyptian descent. She had gorgeous green eyes, long silky hair, beautiful burnt brown skin color, and a very fit body with all the assets. I was working at Lowes (my summer and first real job) when I first met her. I was assigned to help her find what she needed for that day. I walked her to the car, and she had a lot of stuff to load. I loaded her car and came to find out that they were going to be delivering some items to her house, and I was working in the delivery department that day. My coworker and I went over to her house, and when we got there, we saw a huge house. I mean it is laid to the max. Since the woman was fairly young (I believe she was twenty-four at the time), I figured she still lived with her parents.

We dropped her items off, and the whole time, this woman and I are laughing, joking, and flirting, I'm thinking she is really cool a great person to "kick it" with sometimes. While my co-delivery guy was at the truck, she gave me her number and offered to pick me up after work and take me home (I did not have a car at the time), so being the man that I was, I didn't turn her down because I knew where this is going. I went over to the house with her later, and we ended up having sex, and she brought up that she would love to see me again. I think to myself that this is going down a road I don't like because maybe she wants a relationship, but I obliged. This activity continued for about a week when she said she wanted to stop. I'm fine with that because I'm not emotionally attached to her in that way. I just thought she was a really cool girl, and we had a "friendly" relationship. It was close to the end of summer and almost time for me to go back to school when she texted me out of the blue. She wanted to know if I had left for school already or still working. I told her I had already quit and was leaving soon.

The next day, my boss called me and wanted to know if I wanted a few extra hours before I left for school, and I did not have anything to do, so I just went in and worked a full shift. Since I had already quit, my supervisor put me on deliveries for the day, so I did not have to work in a department that day. As we were delivering, we stopped at this woman's house that I was having encounters with, and as we pulled up, a short muscular Hispanic man was waving at us as to stop there. Now I've been to this woman's house a lot of times, but I did not ever see this man. Like I mentioned earlier, I just thought she lived with her parents. Then it dawned on me. Yes, this woman was married, and though I found out later that they were getting a divorce because he had gotten a woman pregnant outside of his marriage, I still felt shame. This was crazy. I felt so guilty because of how my family was broken up. I did not want to be a part of an affair whether I knew about it or not. Yet, the signs were there, if I had paid attention. I felt sick to my stomach for the rest of the summer. When I got on that plane a few days later, I felt that I could end up in a place that would haunt me for the rest of my life. In the back of my mind, I knew that what I was doing may not had been the right way to live, but sex felt good, and I was enjoying myself too much.

Sold Out, the Playboy Experience

I was a lost soul. I didn't have any regard for the sexual lifestyle that I was living. I was responsible as far as getting HIV testing and STD checkups but irresponsible because I was having unprotected sex and having no regard for women and their feelings. During my sophomore year, I went completely crazy. At this point in my life, I had never gotten into pornography, but the sexual tension was so strong that at times when I could not get to a woman, I watched pornography and masturbated. Not too long into the year, I got involved with an individual at school that had worked for the college. We were always friends, but after a few late nights hanging out, things suddenly turned physical. We knew that the relationship would never go anywhere, but I found myself getting a bit jealous when she would talk to other guys. It was a weird feeling because I did not even like her enough to want to date her. To some degree, I internally wanted something more but was so deep into what I was doing that I could not see how to stop having sex. Ultimately, things got real messy with the women that I was sexually seeing regularly that we ended up stopping our interaction. She started desiring more than I was willing to give, and I was beginning to shut her out of my life. Our encounters lasted well over a year, off and on.

I did not go home the summer of my sophomore year and decided to stay and room with roommates of mine because of our plans to work and workout during the summer at the school because we had just gotten a new coach and was ready to try to turn the program around. Ironically, I did not have any interaction with women as much that summer. As I look back, the only women I was sexual with was the young lady who worked for the college.

I had always been connected to my roots in some way, shape or form, and I found myself listening to gospel music again, catching short sermons of people on television, and even opening my Bible that summer. I had cut down on the drinking and cut out smoking all together. I was never really into smoking. Actually, if I'm honest, smoking was just one of the things that I did because everyone else did it. Even with all that said, it was clear that my mind had been fully entangled in pornography. It would get to the point that I would watch it continually throughout the day as if I was watching television. I was never really a fan of it, but what had me gripped was the fantasy that came with it. The idea of that though I was not actually with the women in the scenes, I could envision myself with them, which made it real to me. I would have moments when I wouldn't watch it for periods of times either because I was too busy, or I was sleeping with my friend every day. Nevertheless, if I had downtime throughout the day, my mind was cluttered with pornographic images, and to some degree, it took over my mind so much that the things that I was watching I wanted to incorporate in my sexual encounters. The more I watched porn, the more I desired the fantasy of being with women.

There were times I could not wait to get off work or wait to get done with a workout to get home and watch porn. It was that summer that pornography had gripped me and was not going to let go. It is at this point in my life that I had fully accepted that I was addicted to sex, but it was okay to me. I was going to be this way until I got married, and maybe things would change after that. Little did I know this disease was going to hunt me for many years.

Stole My Heart

I had been in college for a while and have made a name for myself. From the outside looking in, I was the respectable young man who for the most part carried myself well around campus. I was respectful to my professors, was a decent student, and had good relationships with individuals in administration. Yet, secretly I was in a perverse battle with my mind. At this point, I had been sexually involved with women whose names I could not remember, and I rarely felt remorse about it.

I was excited about the new year though. New coach, fresh start, new year, and new freshman women to flirt with. I was still involved with the young lady, but at the moment, she had begun seeing another guy, and we had not had an encounter in sometime. At the college that I attended, the male wing halls had "sister" wing halls with the ladies, and at the beginning of the year or sometime in the first semester, we would get together with our sister wing and have an activity. This year was a year they decided to have the males come over, and they cooked up an evening breakfast while we mingled and played mixer games. It was this night that I noticed a young lady who I thought was gorgeous and her body, *oh my goodness!* She had the nerve to be a curvy girl from the waist down and wear this pajama that showcased her best physical asset. I did not approach her that night but best believed I was going to hit that. Around this time, Facebook had become a national phenomenon, and everyone had a page, so I requested her as a friend and began to message her back and forth. She had met me at the mixer, so she knew who I was, but as we began to talk, I noticed that she was a bit different. I was trying to flirt with her, and she wasn't really playing into it. She did say that she thought I was attractive, but outside of that, she wasn't paying me any attention on a more intimate level. Everything I talk about with her was on a "need to know" basis. I would ask her a question, and before she would respond, she would say, "Why you need to know that?" Man, it was rough.

Noticing that she was not really interested in anything I had to say I took a chance anyway and asked if she would like to hang out sometime. She accepted my request, and we went out a few times after that night. After that, things kind of took off faster than I thought they would. In fact, I was not ready for the level of commitment that I was getting ready to submerse myself into. When it comes to relationships, I always had an "old school" approach to it in that I believed in being in a relationship only for the purpose of seeing if I wanted to marry that person one day. Because of that way of thinking, I did not get into a relationship because I knew I was not ready for the level of responsibility that came with that. The more I hung around this young lady, the more I felt like she was improving me. When I was with her, I did not think about other women, sex, or pornography. It was something that I had been missing for a long time. It was in our long drives, deep conversations, and intimate encounters that I realized that maybe the bachelor lifestyle is not for me or at least has come to an end.

Maybe I was wrong about never being able to get married. Maybe I was wrong about a lot of things. One late night, as we were driving around the small town of McPherson, we came to a stop at this Christmas scenery. The whole week, we had been talking about the idea of having sex soon, but it was never a focus of any of our conversations. She nor I were virgins, but she definitely wasn't as versed as I was in the area of sex. She had only had a couple boyfriends and was not that sexually involved with them as I was with multiple women. We had drove off to a secluded place in the middle of central Kansas, and though we were not planning on having sex, it ended up happening in the car that night. That night felt different. Though it was still wrong based on how I believed and was brought up about how sex should only be in marriage, I did not feel a sense of detachment after it. It was quite the opposite. I felt more attached to her as if there was a strong connection that was made after we had finished. I had no intentions of being with anyone else at that point.

Time passed and we continued to date. I had become an extremely jealous person at this point and demanded a lot of my girlfriend's time—so much that it had begun to cause an amalgam of arguments between us. At this point, we have been having sex once or twice a week, so I began to develop dominance over her that later I realized ultimately tore us apart.

Close to the end of that school year, she had decided she had enough. She had gotten tired of the arguments and the jealous behavior that she decided to call it quits. She told me that in her heart, she did not want to do it, but it had become so mentally and emotionally draining for her that she couldn't handle it any longer. I can't lie and say that it did not affect me. I was emotionally hurt. I did everything in my power to convince her that I would do my best to work on things but to no avail. That night I took a long walk around this lake in town called Wall Park, and I walked and walked and walked trying to understand it all. I didn't really have too much interaction with women for the rest of that school year. All I could think about was her. I felt like a failure, thinking that the one real adult relationship that I had I could not sustain it, or even make to work.

We continued to talk as friends, but there was always this feeling like we were never fully over each other. The summer came, and she returned home for that time. Like I did the previous summer, I stayed and worked. That summer was a really rough one because I found myself drunk on many nights. A few teammates stayed this summer and, almost every weekend, was a drinking social gathering. We had no conscience. That summer, we worked enough to have what we needed but were at this local bar whenever we had a chance. I also began seeing the young lady that worked for the college again that summer. I believed she was on her way out and looking into other options that summer and was not going to be at the college too much longer. Though our encounters was not as intense as they once were in the past and we were not doing it as much as before, it was enough to mess with her feelings and have her thinking that she may be able to have what I once had with my ex-girlfriend. She seemed to be more attached this time around, but all I wanted was someone I could be sexual with. I believed that in the long run she was feeling heat of getting older and wanting that person there that she could settle down with. With me still being so young, I was not necessarily looking for that or at least not with her. Over time, she found a boyfriend and moved on, and we stopped all of our sexual encounters together. She moved out of the state, and until this day, I have not seen or heard from her.

When my senior year came around, my ex-girlfriend had returned for her second year. With that body still looking so right and my great charm, it was hard for either of us to resist each other, and before the third week had begun in school, we were back at it and dating again. It was a bit different. I tried to change my ways and allowed her to express herself freely, but ultimately, the arguing started again. We were back into a very physical relationship. Sex was the only thing that we really had in common. Our physical attraction toward each other was unbelievable, but other than that, we were two very different people. I saw us drifting away, and I really did like her, so I made a vow to try to shape up. I changed the way I talked to her,

I gave her the space she needed, and I decided I was going to try to love her with my whole heart. I thought that if I do it right and go all in with my heart, then we can rid some of the mess that we were going through. So I went for it. I dove in head first and decided I was going to try to love again.

She seemed to like this new me, and for a while things were actually getting better. We were communicating more, having fun, enjoying each other's company. I thought this love thing was finally working out for me. We dated for almost my whole senior year. In fact it was my whole senior year. She had decided that she was going to move back home, and I honored that. My plan was to move out there with her and get my master's at a school there. This was the plan, but I got approached with an interesting proposition. If I had stayed at the college to be a graduate assistant resident director, the school would assist me in getting my master's degree. I knew she wasn't going to stay, and for the most part, we had agreed that it would be okay because she was only three hours away. So I stay get moved into my new living quarters at the college and ready to live the good life. I had my girl, my new job, and the people I loved closest to me rooting me on. Life was good, for about two weeks.

As the summer began, things took yet another turn for the worst. Not seeing her as often would take a toll on me because I was used to being with her all the time. My body would crave her sexually, and I would get frustrated and want to call her and just talk to her. To add to the frustration, she seemed like she was always out or did not have enough time to talk to me on the phone. Things were becoming different. We were not the same couple that we had been. We would have constant arguments about some of the dumbest stuff people can fight over. Honestly, we fought over something that had to do with cheese. It was ridiculous and even fought one time during fourth of July because she had ask me if I wanted to come to the lake with her and I said I couldn't and I was mad because she didn't tell me she was going to the lake. Yes, very dumb. Just because I said I couldn't go didn't mean she wasn't going. So things just boiled over so much that it was a fight every day.

Then I began seeing pictures and things with her friends. Facebook had become iconic at this point, and you could see everybody's business. She was in a lot of pictures with this guy, but I did not make any notion of it. I knew she had friends, and I thought it was no big deal. I was still in the fully sold-out-to-love mind-set, so I became naïve to anything that seemed suspicious. Then one week, while I was at home in California, I tried calling and texting her, and I got no answer. I was actually getting nervous that something had been wrong because we had talked earlier, and of course, that turned into an argument, but we had made up about an hour later, so we were good. The next morning, I called her to see what was going on, and she just went off on me, saying she didn't want to be with me anymore, that she doesn't love me, that I'm not her type of husband. It was bad. I fought tooth and nail to get her to stay in my life. I sent flowers. I told her I would do whatever it took but to no avail. That morning, my mom took me to the airport, and the whole way there, I looked out the window because I did not want her to see the tears flow from my eyes, and once I got through the security, I found a spot in the corner facing a wall, and I just cried. I held my phone to my ear to make it seem like I was on the phone, but no one was talking to me. I was just crying. The more I thought about it, the more I cried. When I got home, I tried to call once again, but nothing was working. She was gone.

To make matters worse, not even a week later, I saw a picture of her kissing another guy (who eventually became her boyfriend) on her Facebook page. It was the same guy that had been in the pictures before. I can't make the conclusion that she cheated on me because that would be unfair, but I can make the conclusion that she left me for him. I know that I wasn't perfect and that I did not always do things right, but I was always loyal, and I always had that hope that things would be alright. I pride myself on being a good person, but at that point, it seemed like being a good person wasn't enough.

God Blocked It

I was distraught. I had no hope. Once again my heart was in a bad place. I did not want to be bothered. I secluded myself to my apartment, and even my friends noticed a significant change in my attitude and behavior. I just wanted to be alone. I felt empty on the inside. I did not want to eat and couldn't sleep. I would take Nyquil to help put me to sleep. I even would take shots of alcohol so I would get drunk and not have any recollection of anything. To me it was more than about my ex. It was the feeling of not being wanted by the person you want so badly. It was the first time since high school I had been in this territory. It all boiled over Dad leaving me for another family, the people I love not loving me back, and that all I had been trying to do was please people in my life but they didn't appreciate it. I was the ultimate target for rejection.

I did not want to feel this pain. I was not in my right mind at all. I told myself that this was it. I was going to kill myself right there in my apartment. I had always kept this really nice blade that I got a while ago, and I began to cut myself. I think I cut myself about two or three times. When I did not feel much pain because of the mental state I was in, I moved the blade up to my chest and began to poke myself with it. With every poke, I got deeper and deeper. Not feeling any pain, I kept at it, and when I finally decided I had enough and was going to go for two BIG thrust to the area of my heart, I heard a knock at my door. It was my good friend and former roommate for three years in college, Patrick. Until this day, I have no recollection what he needed, and I don't think he remembers either, but one thing I do know is when I shut that door, God's hand was on my life.

I could not call my mother because I knew she would freak out, and I didn't want to call my dad, so I looked to my Pastor Herman Hicks. I texted him and told him that I was in a bad state and not sure what I would do next. Being the person that he is, he left church to come see about me. He and a good friend I call Elder D came to see about me. I had attended his church off and on the latter part of my school years and enjoyed his ministry.

A Preacher's Struggle

In all honestly, I did not see our relationship growing to the point that it did and has. I said to myself he must really care about his flock and God's people enough to drive an hour to make sure I was alright (when he was supposed to be in church). He has a heart for the men of God, and it was evident that night. The one thing that he said to me that was so profound was "You will never have peace until you do what God has called you to do." I have never forgotten that statement. I don't know if he saw something in me that night or when I was coming to church, but that resonated with me. As they left, they put some money in my pocket and told me to be encouraged.

That whole night, I pondered the statement my pastor made to me. What was God calling me to do, so I can have the peace that I desired in my life? I began to think back to my youthful days and how I was so passionate about God and how I was sold out for Him. I began to ask myself, what happened to that person? What happened to that hunger? I think it was that night that I found it again. I found myself faithful in church like never before. I was finding my happiness again, but the peace still wasn't quite there. I still would lay awake at night trying to figure out my purpose and why I had to go through what I went through. Then it just came to me. I knew it was the Spirit of God because once I said it to myself, I felt that peace come over me. It was time for me to accept my call into the ministry. Ever since I left home, I realized that I had been running, trying to be a person that I was never supposed to be. I was here to spread the Word of God. Not too long after that night, I told my pastor that I want to go into the ministry and his response was interesting.

The first thing he asked me was if I was sure. I thought that was ironic because you would think that someone in his position would just say, "Good. We need more preachers." Yet, he knew something I didn't know at the time. He just saw me come out of a painful situation, and he did not want me to think that being a preacher could solve that. In fact, I think he wanted to protect me to some degree because if I thought that I had experienced pain and rejection before, there is nothing like the pain and rejection of being a preacher. He knew what I didn't know. So he told me to read 1 and 2 Timothy and then come back to him. I read through both of those letters of the New Testament. I still was pretty confident in God calling me to be a preacher, so I kind of blew off the reading and read with no intent on getting a full understanding. A couple weeks later, I went back to him and said I was convinced I wanted to be a preacher, and he said okay and told me to come to the next ministerial meeting. Like I mentioned before, he knew something I didn't, and I was quickly about to find out what it was.

Alone

Being all excited about this new adventure in my life, I quickly changed my master's degree plan to a ministry degree and started watching sermons of some of the most profound preachers and pastors in the country. I mean I had every T. D. Jakes, Noel Jones, and Rick Warren sermons I could get my hands on. I was taking notes every Sunday in church and observing how to do church. I believe my spiritual father Pastor Hicks is a great organizer and leader, and he always made sure things were in order. So I watch his every move. I would go home and try to practice preaching for when my time came (I had to sit for six months to observe and learn). I would learn sermons by heart so that I could picture myself preaching them in a church. My heart was pure at the same time because for me it wasn't about preaching, it was about helping God's people.

Remember I came from a broken home. My family didn't have much growing up, and the one thing my mother always taught me was to be a good person, so despite my insensitivity to women's emotions, helping people has always been embedded in me. So in whatever I did, I just wanted God to see my heart in it all.

Many things began to change. I stopped hanging out in certain places, my language changed, and I just had a different outlook on life in general. There was nothing else I wanted to do more than serve God. Yet, when I began to let go of these things, my world became very dense. My friends would go out to certain places and do certain things, and I could not do those same things. For the most part, it didn't affect me, but when people started treating me differently when I told them my new position, I realized that my life and relationships with people would no longer be the same.

I did not know ministers at my age that I could really hang with. At this point, all my really close friends had moved away or back home, so I really didn't have anyone to talk to. I tried to build relationships with certain individuals at my church, but it didn't feel genuine. It was not the same connection that I had with my friends from college. So with no one to really talk to and focused on trying to live this life as a preacher, I became lonely. For me, becoming lonely was the worst thing that could happen because I started to look for acceptance and validation from women.

I was really focused on being a preacher, and my first sermon was approaching fast, and the closer I got, the more nervous I got. There was a young lady that I began liking. She was different. She wasn't like the typical women whom I had been involved with before. We had a lot in common, and the more I talked to her the more she grew on me. It is tough to describe our relationship. The attraction was there, but we had very awkward moments. It was almost like she had a fear of being with me because of the position that I was in. We talked for a while, and even went out a few times, but it was clear that she was not interested in having anything more than a friendship. We had our moments over the years, but we could never seem to get past the friends zone or at least she couldn't. She is one of the women I respect the most because she has always been upfront with me, but that doesn't mean that I wasn't affected by her request to just remain friends. I honored that.

Out of the many women I had been with and dated, there will never be one like her in this story. I can say that no woman has ever captivated me like she did, and the weird part is I don't even know why. I realized that I had to move on because we both had very different life goals at that point in our quest for success, at that time in our lives. We tried being friends, but I think we both knew that wasn't realistic. As it is today, we still talk when we see each other and have short text message conversations, but that is the extent of our "friendship," and I believe we are both okay with that. If we would have met later in life when we were both older and more accomplished (early thirties maybe), I'm sure we both would agree that things would have had a better chance of being different.

The nights got long, and my desire to have that special person got stronger—so strong that I began dating women that I knew were not good for me. I would have these one-to-two month relationships that had absolutely no substance to them at all. I tried to circumvent my love life because I saw all of my close friends getting married. It was a struggle for me. I would go home every night wanting to have that one person that I could hold, and they would hold me back. Someone I could tell my day to, most importantly or at least very importantly, someone I could make love to and it actually means something.

Though I was a preacher, I was still having these strong physical feelings. I would do everything in my power to fight them, but I couldn't. By this time, I had preached my first sermon, and I was doing really well in the ministry. I had completed my first master's degree and had accomplished everything I set out to do, but I was empty on the inside. Every woman, I wanted didn't want me back, and the ones who did want me I knew would never last because of their lifestyle and mine as a preacher. So I became frustrated. My frustration led to stress, and ultimately stress led me back into a pornography addiction.

To be honest one of the main reasons I started looking at it again was that I felt this was a way for me to combat the need of having women over for sex. I tried to get out the apartment, workout, keep my mind busy, but whenever I got home, it was like that spirit was there waiting on me, and it was hard to fight. I wanted to be the man of God that he always called me to, but the more I tried to live a holy life, the harder it seemed I fell. There would be times that I would preach a great word to the glory of God, and right after, I would go watch porn and masturbate. Or I would be preparing to speak and masturbate, and when I would get up there, I could feel conviction over me that made me feel like a hypocrite. It was something I felt I could not shake.

Whenever I would have a bad day at work or my finances got low or if another woman decided dating a preacher was not the desire of her heart, I would revert to porn. This time around, it was not about the fantasy or the women. It was simply my stress reliever and peace filter. Though I knew it was wrong, and I felt convicted afterward. I still could not control myself from having occurrences. I would get so frustrated at myself that I focused my anger on God. There were times where I would literally have shouting bouts where I would just yell at God. Why this? Why that? Why did she leave? Why doesn't this person want to be with me? Sure the easy thing would be to say I should have been patient and all that other jazz that sounds good but doesn't feel good. I've had many conversations with people about this, and they all said the same thing: "I understand." Yes, maybe a few years ago, but you getting some on the regular.

Though we hear that it is *not* the same because different people have different degrees of physicality, sexuality, and emotions based on the particular situation. If an individual was to lose a child suddenly rather than a parent seeing death coming from a disease or illness, they both know what it's like to lose a child, but for the most part, it is easier for one to have peace about the death and able to prepare themselves. Well, this is how I felt about individuals who were virgins until marriage and would tell me they "understood" what it was like to live single with these strong sexual feelings.

Though I applaud them for their will to not give in, I took a different path and was used to getting sex when I wanted it and having a variety of women to do it with. It is psychologically proven to be a difference (I don't want to stray too far from the story so I won't deal with that too extensively here but make sure you get my next book, *No Strings Attached*, where I deal with the psychology of conflating sexual addictions and spirituality.

Things really became concerning when I started engaging in a physical relationship with a young lady whom I had dated for a short time. We both knew that it was wrong, but we were caught in a cycle that we could not seem to break. The more we tried to stop sleeping together, the more we had sex. It got to the point where this woman would come to my second job that I worked at overnight, and we would have sex there also. The shame was there, but so was the feeling of the flesh also. I had lost all self-control at this point. Pornography became natural; sex with this woman became a norm, all while preaching the gospel. I didn't want to be alone anymore, so as long as I kept having sex with her, I knew she would always be around, and as long as I was attentive to her emotions, she kept having sex with me.

It got to a point where her emotions were so involved that I knew I had to distance myself from her. Even though I knew this was the right thing to do, she filled that void of being alone many times. Yes, our relationship was very sexual, but we would actually have some really good conversations. We had a connection that was pretty deep, but because of the physicality of our relationship, we could not get past the sex to have a decent relationship. Over time, I knew that this cycle had to get broken, so I decided to text her and tell her that I wanted to cut it off for good. I will admit that there were a few times we slipped up, but eventually we both faded in different directions and ended our three-year sexual relationship.

The nights continued to get long, with no one really to talk to, no one to embrace, and leaving myself to my own perverted thoughts and pornography indulgence. This was a secret that I kept to myself for many years. I would preach and, on those same nights, masturbate. I had thought I tried it all, praying, fasting, talking to pastor on many instances, but I could not shake this sickness. I would beat myself up so much emotionally about it that eventually I just stop fighting it altogether and said it will just be something that I would have to live with.

Struggle Turned Testimony

Time continued to pass by, and I continued in my normal cycle of sexual activities. I had given up on dating and given up on the idea of getting married. I was living this life as a crushed individual that saw no hope. I told myself that I was going to give up on my ministry as well. I never told anybody, but I would purposely miss church as much as I could, so I didn't have to be convicted of anything. I stopped reading my Bible, stopped praying, and even had a bad semester in grad school.

I believe I was at my lowest point during this stretch even more than when I wanted to commit suicide. I would avoid having to preach as much as I could and did not want to be around my friends or family. Everything that I had been through had surfaced back up. Though it may have been unfair, I blamed everything on my father. The one thing I said I would not inherit from him was the greatest battle in my life. I felt his father cursed him, and ultimately he cursed me. I was drowning in debt and seemed like I had no hope. There was a time I literally have had to make choices whether to put gas in my car to get to work or eat that day. Sometimes, all I had to eat for dinner was corn and water literally. I was too prideful to ask for help many times because everyone in my family looked up to me. They saw the degrees and success that I had in school but didn't know that I was at a point of being evicted from my apartment. I hated life but loved my family too much to try to take mine again.

I thought to myself how God could let me go through all of this. Even though I had a struggle, I was still doing my best to be a good person and serve his people. I was faithful and loyal to my pastor, and the women that I did date I did my best to treat them the best I could. I felt that living right was not working for me. I felt like I had no hope left.

It was on a Saturday night when I went to a liquor store and bought two bottles of Vodka (I believe they were forty-ounce bottles), and within three maybe four hours, both bottles were gone. I was mixing it with juice at first but then somewhere within those few hours I started taking straight shots. I completely blacked out for a while.

When I came to my senses, I went to take a shower, and I was still so weak that I just laid in the bathtub while the water ran on me. While in the shower, I was just vomiting nonstop, and I believe I passed out again.

I came to myself again and still balled up in the shower. Then I just started crying. I cried and cried and cried. I felt like a failure. I felt as if I could never be what God called me to be. The next day, I was in church drunk as I could be. I had a hard time focusing on the service, and if I had been on program to do anything, I would have probably vomited in the process. My mind was so jacked up the night before that the money I had initially was going to use to buy food I spent on alcohol, so for the next couple days, I did not eat anything.

Being frustrated at myself about that the only thing, I watched in the span of those two days was pornography. That week I had slept with three different women, but it was on that Friday when I experienced something was different. I went to the woman's house, and we did what we did, and I left. As I was walking to my car, I kept getting this weird anxious feeling.

I hooked my phone up to my car to play music, and I pushed the shuffle button, and the first song that started playing was Kirk Franklin's "Imagine Me," and tears began to roll down my face; then Lamar Campbell's "More than Anything" played right after, and I lost it. I pull over on the side of the road on Interstate 35 and cried for about thirty minutes straight. It was at that moment that I had gotten sick and tired of everything, and I remember vividly that I said, "No more."

I got home, and the first thing I did was fall to my knees and began to ask God to forgive me for everything that I had done and said if this is what I'm called to, then he should show me. I did not know where to look to next. I did not know where exactly He was going to take me, but I was committed to be all in. That Sunday I surrendered everything over to him and vowed that I was going to do my best to live for him completely.

I had started taking my ministry more seriously than I have ever took it before. When I spoke, God was really moving through my ministry. I felt the passion come back. The last time I was this excited about ministry was when I first said I wanted to be a preacher. I felt a sense of myself coming back, the man who my mom had raised, and the same guy that prided himself on being good to people and always doing his best to treat them with love. I had talked with my pastor, but I did not tell him everything, but he assured me that my life and ministry had purpose even though I could not always see it.

Learning to properly deal with rejection from that point on, I knew would be a struggle even more. I found that if I voice my opinions and address hurtful thoughts or things that were done or said about me, then I would free myself from keeping them bottled up. I also noticed that as I began to deal with certain issues that my need to relieve stress sexually was not as potent as they would be when I kept much of my frustrations to myself.

The very thing that once had me trapped was becoming the very issue that was leading to my freedom. A day turned into a week, a week turned into a month, a month turned into three months until I found myself not thinking about it at all. It would be irresponsible for me to say that over the course of the time moving forward that I didn't have strong inclinations to fall back into sexual sin, but the less I focused on it, the easier it became. I made a commitment that I was going to serve God in all that I do, and my character would be what would represent me.

Some of the smallest issues in our life end up taking us into places in our life that we never intended to be. I never wanted to struggle with insecurities.

I never wanted to feel that no one wanted anything to do with me. I never wanted to fall into a mental and physical sickness that would take me to the brink of me losing my mind, but it happened. It is important that we deal with issues as they arise in our lives. The demonic spiritual forces that we will have to war against are too strong for our human nature to take on alone.

It is important that we not wait until the issue becomes "too bad" or public before we decide we need to make a change or find people to help us through the process of healing. I'm not going to be perfect, but if I fall, I refuse to stay down. I can't stay down. You can't stay down because there is too much at stake.

Epilogue

I want to say I deeply appreciate everyone who took the time to read my story. Many people don't understand the struggles of leaders in ministry and how the everyday issues of many weigh a little more when on the shoulders of ministry leaders, let alone Christians in general.

There are constant battles that people face that have the tendency to diminish self-confidence and self-worth. Yet it is important to know that we are all overcomers! I heard a great pastor say, "Being a winner doesn't mean I never lose, it means I win more than I lose. So I may not be undefeated but I am undisputed!"

Sexual sin is an area that can easily entangle a Christian because humans were created to have sexual feelings toward each other. Sex was not created to be perverse; man did that. It was created to be a gift to man to be shared between man and woman in marriage, and though my story did not embody that way of living, it doesn't mean that it was right not to wait until honeymoon night.

Christianity is not about how we feel, it's about obedience. Everything that feels right is not right. If sin didn't feel good or provide some degree of pleasure, who would ever do it? It costs to be a winner. At the same time, I do understand that people struggle with issues, but it's only a struggle if you are trying to be better; if you are not trying and doing it without any conviction of the heart or conscience, you are living in it and it is not a struggle.

If you are a man reading my book and find yourself treating women as I did, it is important to understand that women are timeless; they should be cherished and respected even if they don't always respect themselves. I regret how I treated women from my past and many of them have every right to have anger aimed toward me because I messed some of them up emotionally pretty bad. I have come to realize that in order for me to move forward, I can't allow my past to hold me hostage. I can't take back the things that I've done, but I can control my actions for the future and commit to a changed life.

A Preacher's Struggle

Experiences without growth are worthless, so in every life experience, find a way to learn and grow from it. Don't be a prisoner of your issue that you feel you can't tell anyone about because it may damage your reputation. Set yourself free by exposing the things the enemy wants you to keep bottled up.

Don't allow a secret you are struggling with to get into the hands of someone that wants to see you fail in life; their whole assignment is to sabotage you and your ministry. Free your mind and your heart so you can become a NewU.

Forgive, live, and overcome! God Bless!

Contact

Follow Minister Louis Collins on

Instagram @LMCNewU

Twitter: @louie_lou20

Facebook: New U Ministries

Email: Louiscollins0826@yahoo.com